Spider Wig

M. G. Leonard

Illustrated by Lisa Hilker

Ernst Klett Sprachen
Stuttgart

1. Auflage 1 5 4 3 2 1 | 2023 22 21 20 19

© Ernst Klett Sprachen GmbH, Rotebühlstraße 77,
70178 Stuttgart 2019
Alle Rechte vorbehalten.
www.klett-sprachen.de

Autor: M. G. Leonard

Redaktion: Debby Böhm, Don Haupt
Layoutkonzeption: Maja Merz
Illustrationen: Lisa Hilker
Gestaltung und Satz: Joachim Schrimm, bostext, Friolzheim
Umschlaggestaltung: Maja Merz
Titelbild: Lisa Hilker
Tonregie und Schnitt: custom music, Andreas Nesic, Stuttgart
Sprecher: Paul Newcomb

Druck und Bindung: Salzland Druck, Staßfurt

Printed in Germany
ISBN 978-3-12-542647-4

Contents

Worte mit einem * sind unten auf der Seite übersetzt.

Klett-Augmented

Zu dieser Geschichte gibt es auch eine Hörbuchversion und einen Wortschatztrainer, auf die du mit der Klett-Augmented-App zugreifen kannst. Um das Hörbuch abzurufen bzw. herunterzuladen, musst du zuerst die Klett-Augmented-App installieren. Halte dann die Kamera deines Smartphones oder Tablets über die Titelseite (S. 1) des Buches, um sie zu scannen. Im Anschluss kannst du das Hörbuch herunterladen.

Um den Wortschatztrainer zu benutzen, musst du jeweils die erste Seite von jedem Kapitel scannen. Dann erhältst du Zugang zu den Übungen.

Klett-Augmented-App kostenlos downloaden und öffnen

Bildererkennung starten und **diese Seite** scannen

Medien laden, direkt nutzen oder speichern

Folgende Abkürzungen werden in den Worterklärungen verwendet:

etw.	etwas	inf	informal
jdn.	jemand/en	sb	somebody
		sth	something

1
Friday, 13th of June – 6 a.m.

If you are reading this, I am dead.

Calvin Porcus has challenged me to a fight. This is a fight I cannot win. Calvin Porcus has sworn* to hammer me into the ground. Here are the last wishes of an innocent* thirteen-year-old boy – who deserved* to live.

The Last Will* and Testament of Morris Mills
- Tell my family that I love them.
- If Holly Adams is still alive, tell her that I am very sorry for telling Calvin it was her idea about his name. That was wrong and cowardly*.
- Let Holly Adams have any of my fossils or books or anything that she wants from my bedroom as an apology*. If she is also dead, then give them to my friend Harold.
- My little sister, Sukie Mills, can have my savings of £376.56 to put towards her university education, but not to spend on dolls*. Dolls scare me.

---

to swear *schwören* | innocent *unschuldig* | deserved *es verdient haben* | last will *Letzter Wille, Testament* | cowardly *feige* | apology *Entschuldigung* | doll *Puppe*

– Don't let anyone from school come to my funeral*, as they all cheered when Calvin Porcus said he was going to kill me.

It's a terrible tragedy that I had to die because I knew Latin. Well to be precise, just because I translated Calvin Porcus' name from Latin into English. Surely, that can't be considered a crime?! It's not my fault* that his name means 'Bald* Pig'. If I were good at punching and kicking people, then I would still be alive – but I am not. Is it wrong to be bad at fighting and good at maths? I wanted to be a doctor when I grew up, I wanted to cure cancer* and now that won't happen. This cruel life has taught me that being small, bookish and unable to hurt people will get you killed.

You should think about these things when Calvin Porcus is in court* and the jury* are deciding his prison sentence*. Yes, he's still a child, but Calvin Porcus may have murdered the person who was going to cure cancer.

Goodbye cruel world.

Morris

funeral *Trauerfeier* | fault *Schuld* | bald *kahl, glatzköpfig* | to cure cancer *Krebs heilen* | in court *vor Gericht* | the jury *die Geschworenen* | prison sentence *Gefängnisstrafe*

Morris wrote his name at the bottom of the page and nodded*. He didn't know what a will looked like, as he'd never seen one, but this felt right. He didn't have many things to leave behind, but he felt better after writing it all down. He took off his glasses, rubbed his eyes and then put them back on.

He folded up the piece of paper and put it on his bed. When he didn't come home after school, his parents would look for him up here in his bedroom and find it.

He got up with a sigh*. He was already wearing his white school shirt and black trousers. He tied his blue and gold tie around his neck and pulled on his black blazer with the blue and gold crest* on the top pocket. Then he wriggled his arms through his leather bag, so that it sat on his back, against his shoulder blades*. Taking one last look around his bedroom, Morris stepped over to his precious* shelf of fossils. He picked up a large golden rock, put it into his pocket, turned and walked out the door.

2
Friday, 13th of June – 7 a.m.

A figure dropped out of the tree he was walking towards and Morris screamed.

'You're up early,' Holly Adams stood up and put her hands on her hips*. 'Trying to avoid* someone? Me, maybe?'

Morris jumped back in shock, his hands on his chest*. 'You nearly gave me a heart attack.'

'I need to talk with you Morris Mills.' Holly moved her head and her blond ponytail swished like the tail of an angry horse.

'I know, um, I'm sorry, I was...'

'Calvin Porcus and his gang came to my grandad's garden after school yesterday and trampled all over his vegetables. They're mashed* now.'

'Oh no!' Morris's mouth fell open. 'I'm so sorry.'

'Now, I wonder, why would they do that?' Holly asked.

hip *Hüfte* | to avoid *aus dem Weg gehen* |
chest *Brust(-korb)* | mashed *püriert*

'It's my fault,' Morris admitted*, looking down at the ground and feeling terrible. 'Calvin grabbed me in the playground. He asked me who had started the rumour* about his name. You know that it means 'Bald Pig' when translated from Latin.'

'Bald Pig?' Holly laughed. 'Does it? That's brilliant.'

'I take a Latin class after school. I found that out myself.' Morris shrugged*. 'I thought it was funny, so I told my friend Harold. I didn't realise he'd tell everyone. When Calvin grabbed me, I was too scared to admit that it was my fault that everyone was laughing at him, so I told him it was you.'

'You told him it was me?' Holly shook* her head. 'Why did you do that?'

'I didn't know people would write it on the desks in our classroom. I mean, I would never write all over other people's property*.' He shook his head. 'When he grabbed my blazer and lifted me up off the floor, your name popped out of my mouth.' He stared at Holly's angry face through

to admit *zugeben* | rumour *Gerücht* | to shrug *mit den Schultern zucken* | to shake (shook, shaken) *schütteln* | property *Eigentum*

his glasses. 'I think I did it, because you're the only person who isn't afraid of him.'

Holly's face made a series of odd* expressions* and Morris wondered if she was going to kill him before Calvin could. That wouldn't be so bad, although he hadn't thought of this in his will. He didn't want her to get his stuff if she was the one who killed him. 'I'm sorry about your grandfather's vegetables. I really am.' He put his hand in his pocket, pulled out his special stone and offered it to her. 'Here, you can have this.'

'Pretty!' Holly took the rock. 'What is it?'

'Pyrite. Fool's Gold*,' Morris said. 'It isn't valuable*, but it is meant to bring you good luck and protect* you.'

'Why are you carrying it around in your pocket?'

'Because Calvin Porcus is going to kill me today, and I was hoping that the pyrite would protect me. Maybe it could create a force field or make Calvin sick so that he can't come to school for a week or...'

---

odd *seltsam* | expression *(Gesichts-)Ausdruck* | fool's gold *Katzengold* | valuable *wertvoll* | to protect sb/sth *jdn./etw. schützen*

'Hang on* a minute,' Holly interrupted*, 'if you told him it was me that came up with the pig name, why is he going to kill you?'

'Because Mr Tallow, our maths teacher, asked me what was going on and I explained it in front of the whole class. Now, Mr Tallow calls Calvin 'Mr Pig' to get his attention* if he's talking during maths, and the name seems to have stuck. Everyone's calling Calvin Mr Pig now, even the teachers. So, you see, I have to die.'

'Someone says they'll kill you and all you do is walk towards your doom* with a stone in your pocket and no plans of throwing it?' She handed the stone back to Morris. 'Here, keep it. Sounds like you're going to need it.'

'I couldn't throw a stone at anybody,' Morris gasped*. 'I faint* at the sight of blood, and if somebody got seriously hurt? I could go to prison for that!'

'If you don't throw it, you're the one who'll get hurt and even killed. Calvin is brutal. Did you see what he did to that kid in the year above us?'

to hang on *warten* | to interrupt *unterbrechen* | attention *Aufmerksamkeit* | doom *Schicksal* | to gasp *keuchen* | to faint *ohnmächtig werden* |

'I can't throw it.' Morris pushed his glasses up his nose. 'I don't like violence*. I don't approve* of it.'

'How about teaching people lessons*?'

'Learning is good.'

'I want Calvin Porcus to understand that he can't go around smashing people's vegetables. Especially not my grandad's.'

'You mean revenge*, don't you?' Morris bit his bottom lip.

Holly nodded.

'No, thank-you. I'm not very good at revenge.' He shook his head. 'He who ups* and runs away, lives to fight another day.'

'A coward* who ups and runs away, will get picked on* every day,' Holly replied. 'Anyway, you have no choice*. You got me into this mess*. Now, you're going to do as I say and help me teach Mr Pig a lesson.'

'I don't think you should call him that.'

'Oh, shut up*, Morris!'

---

violence *Gewalt* | to approve *etw. gutheißen* | to teach sb a lesson *jdm. eine Lektion erteilen* | revenge *Rache* | to up *aufstehen* | coward *Feigling* | to pick on sb *auf jdm. herumhacken* | choice *Wahl* | mess *Schlamassel* | Shut up! *Sei still! (Halt's Maul!)*

3

Friday, 13th of June – 7.30 a.m.

'You don't understand.' Morris hurried along beside Holly as she marched to school. 'I can't fight. I'm no good at it.'

'Of course, you are,' Holly replied, not slowing down. 'Look at you.'

Morris stopped and looked down at his skinny* body. He checked to make sure he was wearing his glasses. 'You can see me, right? I mean most people, including* me when I look in the mirror, see a small stick boy with a large head and glasses. This makes me easy to push over and a very good punching ball*.' He blinked. 'As far as I can tell, no one looks at me and sees a gladiator!'

Holly laughed. 'No, you're definitely no gladiator, but you're clever, aren't you?'

'Oh yes,' Morris nodded. 'I'm top of my class in maths, all the sciences, and I'm quite good at the cello.'

'Good, then you can beat Calvin.'

'By playing my cello?' Morris had read that music could tame* the heart of the wildest animals, but he wasn't sure it would work on Calvin Porcus.

'No!' Holly stopped and looked down at him. 'For a clever kid, you are also quite stupid.'

Morris gasped. He did not like being called stupid.

'Muscles and strength* aren't the only things that will win a fight you know,' Holly said.

'They aren't?'

'No.'

'You're thinking we should get weapons*?' Morris's eyebrows shot up.

'Yes,' Holly nodded, carrying on walking. 'We're going to need weapons.'

Morris felt a butterfly of panic fluttering in his chest. 'Um, Holly,' he ran after her. 'I'm thankful for what you are trying to do. I really am. And, I do agree that Calvin would benefit from being taught a lesson, but perhaps we could try reading him some philosophy? I'm afraid I am strictly against knives or guns or any kind of tool* for hurting someone.'

to tame *zähmen* | strength *Kraft, Stärke* | weapon *Waffe* | tool *Werkzeug*

Holly slapped* her hand to her forehead*. 'I don't mean knives or guns, you idiot!'

'You don't?'

'Morris, we are thirteen years old, how would we even get a gun?' She shook her head.

'I don't know, it's just that when you said weapons…'

'Wow!' Holly blinked. 'Perhaps you're not as clever as you think you are.'

'Take that back! Let me just remind you that I am the only child in the history of this school to get 100% in ALL their maths tests.'

'Yeah, but I bet* you don't know how to sit on a chair.'

Morris was puzzled by Holly's response*. Of course he knew how to sit on a chair, although he had to admit, he did have a habit* of falling off them, or sitting down when he thought there was a chair behind him and it turned out there wasn't. Last year, he'd come to the conclusion* that chairs could move of their own will, either* that or other kids were moving them when he wasn't looking. Whatever the truth of the matter,

to slap *hauen, schlagen* | forehead *Stirn* | to bet *wetten* | response *Antwort, Reaktion* | habit *Angewohnheit* | conclusion *Schlussfolgerung* | either … or *entweder … oder*

he couldn't claim to be excellent at sitting on chairs, so he fell silent.

'What happens to you when you get frightened*, Morris?' Holly asked.

'That's a strange question.' Morris frowned*.

'You do get frightened, don't you?'

'All the time!'

'Well, what frightens you?'

'Bigger, more stupid people,' Morris replied, counting on his fingers. 'Heights are awful, and rats. Rats are horrible. And dogs, but not normal dogs, just those that are bigger than a donkey*, because they make me think of wolves. Even if they look friendly, they could accidentally* knock* you over and trample you to death.'

'I have never seen a dog bigger than a donkey,' Holly laughed.

to get frightened *sich erschrecken* | to frown *die Stirn runzeln* | donkey *Esel* | accidentally *aus Versehen* | to knock over *umstoßen*

'No, neither* have I, but if I were to see one, I would be very scared indeed.' Morris nodded. 'Oh, and cottage cheese*!'

'What?'

'Cottage cheese is horrifying*.'

'What happens to you when you see cottage cheese?' Holly asked, interested.

'Whenever I see cottage cheese, I get goose bumps* all over my skin. My mind goes dizzy and I think I'm going to throw up in front of everyone. I can't help it, I make retching* noises.'

'Really?'

Morris nodded.

'What would happen if I fired* cottage cheese at you?'

Morris shuddered* as he imagined the white gloopy* sour substance splattering* across his face. 'I would run away.'

---

neither *weder* | cottage cheese *Hüttenkäse* | horrifying *furchterregend, ekelhaft* | goose bumps *Gänsehaut* | to retch *würgen* | to fire at sb/sth *auf jdn./etw. schießen* | to shudder *zittern, erschaudern* | gloopy *zähflüssig* |
to splatter *spritzen*

'And what would happen if you saw a big rat?'

'Same thing, except I'd probably scream while I ran.'

'Do you think this is a rational response to cottage cheese and rats?'

'Um, well, perhaps not rational, but I can't help it.'

'Well, we all have things that we are scared of, and when we are confronted with them, we stop thinking clearly. And then, we panic.'

'True. So?' Morris screwed up his face* trying to understand what Holly was getting at.

'So, if we can make our enemy panic, then we can beat them in a fight.'

Morris stared up at Holly. 'Oh!'

to screw up one's face *das Gesicht verziehen*

Holly grinned*. 'All we need to do is to find out what Calvin Porcus is afraid of before he fights you after school.'

'What if he's not afraid of anything?'

'Everybody is afraid of something.'

4

Friday, 13th of June – 8 a.m.

As he walked through the school gates, towards his classroom, Morris thought about what Holly had said. Everyone is afraid of something. He felt excited. He'd been so worried about being beaten up by Calvin Porcus that he never even thought about winning the fight himself.

He rushed through the door into his classroom, waving* at Harold, his best friend who sat next to him in most of their classes.

'It's D day,' Harold said.

'What's D day?' Morris frowned.

'Your Death Day,' Harold grinned. 'The day the Bald Pig is going to hammer you into the ground. His words not mine.'

'Ah ha!' Morris held up a knowing finger. 'Wrong! You mean it's L Day.'

'L Day?'

'Learning Day, where Calvin Porcus is taught a lesson.'

'A lesson?' Harold lifted an eyebrow. 'What kind of lesson?'

'The lesson that it's not right to go around bullying people.'

Harold burst* out laughing. 'And who is going to teach him that lesson? You?'

'Yes, me. I'm going to win the fight.'

Harold roared* with laughter and promptly fell off his chair, holding his sides.

'What's going on?' Benji, the boy at the desk in front turned around.

'Oh, this is funny. Listen up, Morris thinks he's going to win a fight with the Bald Pig.'

Benji giggled* and soon everyone in class was turning around and laughing as Harold's comment travelled around the room like wildfire*.

Morris frowned. Why was everyone laughing at him? He was being brave*. He was going to stand up to the school bully and teach him that he couldn't push people around. Nobody in class actually liked Calvin. They were all scared of him. So why were they laughing?

brave *mutig, tapfer*

'I can beat Calvin.' He raised* his voice above the laughter*. 'If we all joined together and stood up to him, then he would stop pushing all of us around.'

Harold was crying tears of laughter.

'What's so funny? Come with me, after school. You'll see. If you join forces* with me then we can all teach Calvin Porcus a lesson.'

'Oh, we'll be there,' Harold said, rolling his eyes. 'We wouldn't miss this for the world.'

Morris stared at the amused faces of his classmates and couldn't understand why they were behaving this way. It was almost as if they wanted him to get killed.

'Listen, all we need to do is to find out what Calvin's scared of and then use it against him,' Morris explained, trying to remember how Holly had put it. 'For example, I'm scared of cottage cheese, so if you wanted to beat me in a fight you could fire cottage cheese at me.'

The class broke out in another wave of laughter. A cheese sandwich flew through the air and hit Morris in the face.

to raise one's voice *lauter werden* | laughter *Gelächter* | to join forces *sich zusammenschließen*

'The Bald Pig isn't frightened of ANYTHING!' Harold said, 'Except maybe a bacon sandwich.'

His classmates hooted* and cackled* as Mr Smythe, their teacher strode in with the morning register* under his arm. He clapped his hands to silence* the room, but even the teacher couldn't stop the giggles completely*.

Harold got back onto his chair. 'I'm going to miss you Morris, you're funny.' He wiped* his eyes.

'But I'm not going anywhere.' Morris had a sinking feeling in his stomach.

'I mean, after the Bald Pig kills you,' Harold grinned. 'Don't worry, I'm going to bring my phone and film the fight for YouTube. Your last moments will make you famous...'

to hoot *prusten, johlen* | to cackle *gackern* | register *Anwesenheitsliste* | to silence *zur Ruhe bringen* | completely *vollständig* | to wipe *(ab-)wischen*

5
Friday, 13th of June – 9 a.m.

Morris was not having a good day. The school seemed to be excited by the big fight and his certain* death. School bully Calvin Porcus paraded through the corridors flexing* his biceps and winking at girls, while they all cheered him on.

certain *sicher* | to flex *anspannen*

'What is wrong with everybody?' Morris wondered. 'They should be on my side. I'm the victim* here.' But everywhere he looked, his classmates turned away from him, as if he were not even there. If he didn't know better, he'd have thought they were on Calvin's side.

His first lesson was history, but Morris only half listened to the teacher, as he tried to understand why, when he'd explained how his classmates could help him beat the school bully and therefore all win, none of them had listened, not even Harold. 'They think I'm a loser,' he realised.

'It's not personal,' Harold explained. 'Think about it. There's no way you can win this fight. The Bald Pig is massive and good at fighting. He enjoys it. You are a bit of a wimp, and you faint at the sight of blood.' He laughed. 'Hey, remember that time when we were playing football and you fainted because you skinned your knee?'

'That was a bad cut. I nearly had to go to hospital,' Morris said. 'I could have bled* to death.'

Harold shook his head. 'There is no way you can win this fight, Morris. I like you, I really do. You're my friend, but I can't be seen to be supporting you, because I don't want to be the next person Calvin Porcus decides to give a D Day.'

'You are not supporting me?' Morris was upset.

'History is the story of the victor*,' the teacher said. 'After a conflict, the victor is the one who gets to tell their version of what happened. The loser's story often disappears*.'

Morris felt like he was talking directly to him. If he lost his fight with Calvin Porcus today, the world wouldn't care about Morris Mills' last will and testament, or how he planned to spend his life curing cancer. They would only know Calvin's story, and they would celebrate his victory.

'Harold,' Morris whispered, 'you know you said you'd film the fight on your phone?'

Harold nodded.

'Did you mean it? Do you promise to come and do that?'

'Just try and stop me,' Harold nodded. 'I reckon* I'll get a million views, easy.'

'Good,' Morris said.

victor *Sieger(in)* | to disappear *verschwinden* | to reckon *meinen, vermuten*

Nobody was going to help Morris against Calvin, except Holly. He decided that he would do his best to get her what she had asked for. He was going to find out what Calvin Porcus was afraid of. And he knew exactly how he was going to do it. His worst enemy had a little sister. In his experience little sisters hated their big brothers. All he had to do was find Mary Porcus and ask her one simple question.

6
Friday, 13th of June – 10 a.m.

'Morris Mills, what do you think you're doing?'

Morris froze*, recognising* the cold voice of the head teacher, Mrs Berk. He slowly turned around to face her, trying to think of a good excuse for being out of class and on his tip-toes looking through the porthole window* in the door to the girls' toilets.

to freeze (froze, frozen) *frieren, hier: erstarren* | to recognise *erkennen* | porthole window *Bullauge*

'I need the toilet, Miss,' he said. This wasn't a total lie, because the moment that he had heard her voice, he realised how desperately* he needed to pee*.

'And you are staring into the girls' bathroom because...?' she left the question hanging in the air above her raised* eyebrows.

'It's closest to my classroom, and I'm really desperate,' Morris replied. 'I thought I might quickly pop into the girls' loos* if they were empty. I was looking through the window to see if anyone was in there.' He blushed*, pleased* that his lie made sense.

'Really?' Mrs Berk didn't sound so convinced*.

Morris nodded, crossing his legs and hopping up and down to demonstrate how much he needed the toilet.

'Well then, in you go.' Mrs Berk gestured* for him to go into the girls' bathroom.

'What?' Morris squeaked*.

---

desperately *dringend* | to pee *(inf) pinkeln* | raised *gehoben* | loo *(inf) Klo* | to blush *erröten* | pleased *zufrieden* | convinced *überzeugt* | to gesture sb to do sth *jdm. deuten, etw. zu tun* | to squeak *quietschen*   31

'If you need the toilet that urgently, then please, go ahead. I will stand here and make sure no girls enter while you are in there.'

'Oh! Okay. Thank you!' Morris backed towards the door. 'Are you sure?'

'I'm sure,' she nodded.

Morris had never been inside the girls' bathroom before. It smelt very clean. There was even toilet paper. He looked up, the ceiling was clear. In the boys' bathroom, the ceiling was plastered* with chewed-up* globs* of toilet paper that had been fired up there with straws*.

Morris needed to pee but didn't want to go to the bathroom in here. He locked himself into a cubicle*, counted to one hundred and then flushed*. He came out and washed and dried his hands.

When he left the bathroom, Mrs Berk was standing beside a group of girls. They all stared at him.

'Hi!' Morris waved at them nervously.

---

to be plastered with *bedeckt sein mit* | chewed-up *zerkaut* | glob *Klumpen* | straw *Strohhalm* | cubicle *Kabine* | to flush *spülen*

'Just had to go to the girls' loos eh?' a girl called Nancy jeered*.

'Bet it was one of his dying wishes,' another girl sniggered*.

'Mr Mills was desperate, weren't you Morris?' Mrs Berk's face was blank*, but Morris felt that she was enjoying his humiliation*. 'So desperate he couldn't walk around the corner to the boys' bathroom. He just had to use yours.'

'Ew, gross*!' Nancy wrinkled her nose*, 'Mrs Berk, could you please ask the caretaker* to clean the toilets with extra bleach*.'

'I'm sure he always does. Now Mr Mills, back to your classroom please.'

Morris put his hand into his jacket pocket as he hurried back to his classroom. He held on to the fool's gold. So far it wasn't bringing him any luck at all.

He'd been hovering* around outside the girls' bathroom, looking for Calvin Porcus' little sister Mary. If anyone knew what Calvin was afraid of,

to jeer *verspotten* | to snigger *kichern* | blank *leer hier: ausdruckslos* | humiliation *Erniedrigung* | gross *eklig, widerlich* | to wrinkle one's nose *die Nase rümpfen* | caretaker *Hausmeister* | bleach *Desinfektionsmittel* | to hover around *herumlungern*

it would be her. Sukie, his own little sister, found every possible chance to hold cottage cheese under his nose. He was certain that Mary would be the same. Sisters enjoyed annoying their big brothers. But, until he found Mary Porcus, he was going to have to ask every person he bumped into, whether they knew of any fears or phobias that Calvin Porcus might have.

'I heard that Calvin is scared of snakes,' he said to a group of children in the corridor at break time.

'I don't think so,' one of them replied. 'Last year he brought a picture into class from his visit to the zoo. He had a giant albino python around his neck and he was smiling.'

'Someone told me that Calvin Porcus is afraid of rats,' Morris said to three girls jumping rope in the playground.

'Then why was he boasting that he killed three with a shovel*?' one girl replied as she jumped up and down.

shovel *Schuufel*

'Hey, is it true that you like to sneak* out of class and go into the girls' loos and pee on the seats?' one of the girls swinging the rope said.

"No!' Morris was shocked. 'Absolutely not.' Being a secret-hunter* was turning out to be much more difficult than he'd thought.

7

Friday, 13th of June – 11 a.m.

The morning was coming to an end and Morris was no closer to finding out what Calvin was afraid of. He had asked everyone in his classes, including the teachers, and they had all said the same thing.

'Calvin Porcus is fearless*,' Mrs Dingle the geography teacher said. 'He is not even afraid of homework.' She smiled, 'He always turns it in* on time*.'

Morris began to worry. Maybe Holly was wrong. Maybe not everyone was afraid of something. What would happen if he failed in his mission? Could Holly still teach Calvin a lesson, even if he wasn't afraid of anything? Was it Morris' Death Day after all?

'Mr Mills do you have an answer for us?' Mr Tallow the maths teacher asked.

Morris jumped. He hadn't been paying attention. In maths! His favourite subject. What was wrong with him? 'I'm very sorry Mr Tallow, I wasn't listening.'

'I beg your pardon?' Mr Tallow turned around and stared.

'I was miles away,' Morris admitted and then smiled. 'Could you please repeat the question for me?'

The classroom rippled with giggles as Mr Tallow's face went purple.

'I suppose* you have something more important to do than listen to a boring explanation of Pythagoras' theorem?'

'Oh no. I understand Pythagoras' theorem,' Morris blinked.

'You do, do you?' Mr Tallow crossed his arms.

'Yes,' Morris nodded proudly.

'Then what is the answer to my question?'
Mr Tallow raised his bushy eyebrows.

'But, I don't know what the question is?' Morris spluttered*.

More giggles.

to suppose *annehmen* | **to splutter** *entrüstet hervorstoßen*

'I'm waiting, Mr Mills.'

Morris looked around, hoping someone would help him by mouthing* the question, but nobody moved. 'This is unfair!' He banged his hands on the desk in frustration. 'You know I could answer the question if you told me what it was.'

The classroom fell silent and Morris got a sinking feeling in his stomach. Mr Tallow had a quick temper*.

'That's a half hour detention* for you, Mr Mills. Today, after school. Go to the English block, Room 5C.'

'WHAT?!' Morris cried. 'But Mr Tallow, that's not fair. I've never had a detention in my life! Please take a moment and rethink your decision.'

'I have. Your detention will now be an hour, and I'd keep my mouth shut for the rest of this lesson if I were you. Unless*, of course, I ask you a question, in which case, be sure to have the right answer.'

to mouth *etw. lautlos sagen* | to have a quick temper *sich schnell aufregen* | detention *Nachsitzen* | unless *außer*

There was a low guttural* laugh as Calvin Porcus enjoyed Morris's outrage*. He raised his hand. 'I know the answer Mr Tallow.'

Morris stomped* away from his maths class feeling that the whole world was against him. This was not only going to be the last day of his life, it also seemed like it was going to be the worst.

At lunchtime he followed the crowd of hungry children to the dinner hall. He pulled the fool's gold out of his pocket as he passed a dustbin*. The rock was no help at all. He dropped it into the bin with a clang.

'Hey you!'

Morris turned to see Mary Porcus, Calvin's little sister, walking towards him, flanked by two friends. All three girls had long blond hair that flew backwards as they strutted* forwards. A flicker of hope* sparked up in his chest. 'Hi Mary,' he stepped forward, 'you're just the person I was looking for. My name is...'

guttural *kehlig* | outrage *Empörung* | to stomp *stampfen* | dustbin *Mülleimer* | to strut *stolzieren* | flicker of hope *Hoffnungsschimmer*

39

'Dead Meat.' Mary finished his sentence. Her friends giggled.

'Um, I was wondering if you could help me.' Morris could already tell that this conversation was going wrong. 'I'm doing a survey* on fears and phobias, collecting information from as many students as possible, and I wanted to ask you, is your big brother, Calvin, afraid of anything?'

Mary lifted her chin*, pretending* to be thinking about his question. She levelled an absurdly confident* look at him and said. 'Calvin is fearless. There is absolutely nothing that scares him.'

'Are you sure?' Morris persisted*. 'Heights maybe? Big dogs? Cottage cheese?'

'No!' Mary snorted*. 'Who on earth is afraid of cottage cheese?'

'Oh, nobody, I was just wondering,' Morris said.

Mary stepped forward and grabbed his school tie, yanking* his face down towards hers. 'You're the kid that told everyone my brother was a bald pig.' She grabbed his ear and twisted* it hard.

survey *Umfrage* | chin *Kinn* | to pretend *so tun als ob* | confident *selbstbewusst* | to persist *beharrlich bleiben, insistieren* | to snort *schnauben* | to yank *heftig ziehen* | to twist *verdrehen*

'OW! Um, yes,' Morris squealed*. 'It was an unfortunate* mistake.'

'It was, for you. Do you know what people are calling me now?'

'Um,' Morris smiled hopefully, 'lovely pig?'

'Piglet* runt*.'

'That's, erm, cute*?' Morris's eyes were watering.

'No, it is not.' Mary snarled*.

'OUCH!' Morris yelped* as she twisted his ear harder. 'You're hurting me.'

---

to squeal *kreischen* | unfortunate *bedauerlich* | piglet
Ferkel | runt *schwächstes Tier im Wurf* | cute *süß, niedlich* |
to snarl *knurren* | to yelp *jaulen*

'My big brother takes good care of me. If anyone ever upsets* me, he makes sure they never do it again.' She let go of his ear. 'I'm glad Calvin's going to kill you today, because if he wasn't going to kill you, I'd have to do it myself.' She released* his tie and Morris stumbled* backwards.

'I'm terribly sorry if I've upset you,' Morris gabbled* rubbing his hurting ear. 'I really didn't mean to.' He blinked at her through his glasses. 'Calling you piglet runt is awful.'

Mary turned around and looked at Morris over her shoulder. 'I'm really going to enjoy watching you get beaten up later,' she said as she and her friends walked away giggling.

to upset sb *jdn. beleidigen, verärgern* | to release *freilassen, loslassen* | to stumble *stolpern* | to gabble *nuscheln*

8

Friday, 13th of June – 12 p.m.

'Did I just see Mary Porcus pushing you around?' Harold ran up to Morris. 'She's only eleven!'

'We were having a chat,' Morris coughed, trying to think of a way to change the subject.

'It didn't look like a very friendly chat,' Harold said.

'Yeah, well, Mary doesn't like me very much.'

'No?'

'No,' Morris frowned. 'People have started calling her piglet runt.'

Harold shook his head. 'You are so dead.'

Morris had to admit that his friend was right. Things looked bad. Mary had been his last hope of finding out what Calvin was afraid of. 'I don't suppose you've managed to find out what Calvin's afraid of?' he asked Harold.

'Yeah, I have actually.'

'Really?'

'Yeah, I asked him. He reckons he might be afraid if he was attacked by a shark or a T-Rex.'

Morris' flicker of hope died. For a short moment, he wondered if it would be possible to find a shark to help him in his fight with Calvin, but even with his high intellect and wild imagination*, he realised that wasn't going to happen. 'You're right,' he looked at Harold, 'I'm dead.' He sighed*, 'Shall we go get lunch?'

'Oh, sorry,' Harold looked at the floor, 'but you can't sit at our table today. Benny has your seat now.'

'Benny? Benny who smells of fish and spits* when he eats? You're ditching* me for Benny?'

Harold nodded, still looking at the floor. 'We took a vote*, and no one wants Calvin to think that you are our friend. It's dangerous. If he sees you eating with us, we might be next on his list. That's why I came over to talk to you. To let you know. You're going to have to sit with someone else.'

imagination *Fantasie, Vorstellungskraft* | to sigh *seufzen* | to spit *spucken* | to ditch sb *jdn. abservieren* | to take a vote *abstimmen*

'But who is going to want to sit with me?' Morris squeaked.

'Yeah, well, sorry. See you around,' Harold mumbled* as he walked away.

Morris looked out across the dining hall to the table where he sat to eat his lunch. And there, in his place, Benny was sitting eating his fish paste sandwiches and smiling happily. This day was going from bad to worse, but if he was about to be brutally beaten up, he was going to make sure he got a last meal. He joined the lunch queue and picked up a tray*. When he got to the dinner ladies, he chose the sausage and mashed potatoes*.

'Do you think I could have an extra sausage?' Morris smiled sweetly at the grumpy* woman as she dropped a dollop* of mash onto his plate. 'This could be the last meal I eat before I die.'

'Three sausages per child,' the dinner lady barked, shoving his plate at him.

to mumble *murmeln* | tray *Tablett* | mashed potatoes / mash *Kartoffelpüree/-brei* | grumpy *schlecht gelaunt* | dollop *Klacks, Schlag*

Morris sighed, picked up a drink and a pot of fruit and paid for his lunch. He stood at the side of the hall looking out over the lunch tables, trying to find a free seat.

'There you are,' a voice came from behind him. It was Holly carrying a tray of food. 'C'mon* let's sit over there at that empty table,' she pointed. 'Everyone is acting like I have the plague* today, thanks to you and your big mouth.'

Morris followed Holly to the free table, relieved* to have somebody to sit with.

Holly put her tray down on the table and sat down, immediately scooping* mashed potato into her mouth with a dessert spoon.

'Where are your sausages?' Morris asked as he sat opposite.

Holly swallowed*. 'I'm a vegetarian, so I get extra potato, cabbage* and some baked beans. So, come on then.' Holly nodded her head at him. 'What have you found out? What is the Bald Pig afraid of?'

c'mon *short form of* come on | plague *Pest* | relieved *erleichtert* | to scoop into one's mouth *sich in den Mund schaufeln* | to swallow *schlucken* | cabbage *Kohl*

'Um,' Morris looked up at the ceiling, 'I have it on good authority* that Calvin would run away if attacked by a shark and he might be scared of T-Rexes if they existed. But, um,' he blinked and stabbed* his fork into a sausage, 'it would appear that he is not afraid of anything else.'

9

Friday, 13th of June – 2 p.m.

Morris went through the afternoon in a daze*.
No one wanted to talk to him and that was
fine by him. They had a double art class in the
afternoon. The project was to create a picture
that expressed an emotion*. Morris found
himself cutting out pictures of human skulls*
from a magazine and sticking them onto the
bottom of his piece of paper.

'After I'm killed, people will look at this,' he
thought. 'This will be my last piece of art on
planet earth. People will shake their heads and
say it was a tragedy that someone so talented
should die so young.' In his mind he could hear
the voice of an art critic: 'You can tell from Morris
Mills' use of the human skull as terrain* that he
understood we will all be food for worms.'

After his lunch with Holly, he was pretty certain
that this was the day he was going to become
worm food. He was glad that he'd written his will
this morning.

in a daze *benommen* | emotion *Gefühl* | skull *Totenkopf* |
terrain *Gelände*

48

Holly hadn't seemed surprised by Morris's failure*
to find Calvin's fear. She'd said that people hide
what they are frightened of, for fear of being
laughed at. Morris wondered why he didn't hide
his own fears and thought that maybe he should.
Holly had told Morris that after school, he was
to provoke Calvin and make him angry by being
rude* and cheeky* and then to run to meet her
at the gate to her grandad's garden.

'If we choose the battle ground, then we have an
advantage*,' she'd said.

Morris had nodded, but only because he felt
there was more chance of a grown up stepping in
and saving his life in Holly's grandfather's garden,
than if he was getting beaten up in the small park
behind the school, which was where most fights
took place.

Usually, children would gather* on the
roundabout, swings and climbing frame* to
chant and jeer while two angry students hit
and pushed each other until one of them had a
bloody nose or a black eye*.

failure *Versagen, Scheitern* | rude *unverschämt* | cheeky
frech | advantage *Vorteil* | to gather *(ver-)sammeln* |
climbing frame *Klettergerüst*

Morris never went to the park after school. The sight of violence made him feel dizzy* and sick. He hated fighting. He shook his head. How had he got himself into a fight with the biggest kid in school? He wished he had kept his stupid big mouth shut.

Morris grabbed a paintbrush and dipped* it first in the red paint and then in the black, smearing* streaks* of both colours across the sky above his landscape of skulls. He took a pen and wrote in the bottom right hand corner.

HELL* ON EARTH by Morris Mills

The bell rang. That was it. The school day was over.

Morris grabbed his backpack and ran as fast as he could to the English block and classroom 5C for his detention. He knew he'd be safe in there for one more hour. He knocked on the door.

'Hello Morris,' Mrs Burn ushered* him to a desk that had a dictionary and a piece of lined paper sitting on it. 'I must admit I was quite surprised to see your name on the detention list. Sit yourself down. I'd like you to select* one word

black eye *blaues Auge* | dizzy *schwindelig* | to dip *ein-tauchen* | to smear *schmieren* | streak *Streifen* | hell *Hölle* | to usher sb to a seat/desk *jdn. an seinen Platz/Tisch führen*

50

HELL ON EARTH
by Mom's Mills

from each letter of the alphabet and copy out the word and its meaning.'

Morris nodded. He'd had Mrs Burn for English when he was younger and felt ashamed* to be in her detention class. She didn't teach the upper school. He looked around her classroom. There were written assignments* on the walls from her own class about what they'd done in the Easter holiday.

The window showed an emptying playground, as the children without detention went home. Morris couldn't help noticing* that a crowd of kids had gathered by the gate. They were waiting for someone. His mouth went dry. They were waiting for him.

to select *aussuchen, auswählen* | to feel/be ashamed *sich schämen* | assignment *Aufgabe* | to notice *bemerken*

10

Friday, 13th of June – 4 p.m.

'Do anything you can to make Calvin chase* you,' Holly had said to Morris at lunch. 'You've got to make him really angry. Angry people don't think straight*.'

Morris stared at the open page of his dictionary not seeing the words. His stomach was churning*. He felt sick and afraid. He wanted to do as Holly said, but he wasn't sure how to make Calvin angry. And what if he couldn't run fast enough? He only had short legs. It could all backfire*. His heart was beating so hard in his chest that he wondered whether the other two kids in the classroom could hear it.

Someone must have told the children around the school gate about Morris' detention because they were crossing the playground and coming towards the English block with mean* faces and hands in their pockets or balled up fists*.

to chase *jagen* | to think straight *klar denken* | His stomach was churning. *Ihm drehte sich der Magen um.* | to backfire *nach hinten losgehen* | mean *gemein* | fist *Faust*

Morris's eyes flickered to Mrs Burn. The teacher was busy marking* student's work and didn't look up.

The children outside approached* the classroom silently. Calvin was standing in the middle of the group, almost a head taller than any other kid. He looked into the classroom, locked eyes with* Morris and drew his finger across his throat*.

'Make him really angry,' Holly's voice sounded* in Morris's head.

But how? Morris racked his brains* and before he had time to think about what he was doing, he grinned at Calvin, pushed his nose up into a piggy snout*, stuck out his tongue* and slapped his own forehead. 'Bald Pig!' he mouthed. All the other children turned to look at Calvin to see how he'd react.

Calvin's jaw* had dropped open, but now he snapped it shut*. His forehead wrinkled like gathering seas before an angry storm. He lifted two clenched* fists as a challenge to Morris.

to mark *benoten* | to approach *sich nähern* | to lock eyes with *genau in die Augen schauen* | throat *Hals* | to sound *klingen* | to rack one's brains *sich den Kopf zerbrechen* | snout *Schnauze* | tongue *Zunge* | jaw *Kiefer* | to snap shut *zuklappen* | clenched *geballt*

'Morris Mills, what do you think you're doing?' Mrs Burn's voice turned Morris's head, his finger still pushing up his nose.

'Monkeying around* to impress* your friends is only going to make your detention longer,' she said.

'No, I... I mean.'

'How many words have you written out?' She looked pointedly* at his blank piece of paper.

'Err,' Morris looked at his own empty page and then over at the other two children. Their pages were already nearly full. 'Sorry, Miss.' He turned the pages of the dictionary.

to monkey around *herumalbern* | to impress
beeindrucken | pointedly *gezielt, bewusst*

'I'm done, Mrs Burn,' the girl from the year above him said, holding her page up.

'That was quick, Edith,' Mrs Burn frowned.

'I chose short words,' the girl shrugged. 'Can I go now?'

Mrs Burn nodded. 'Okay Edith, but I don't want to see you in detention again.'

'Thanks, Miss.' Edith stood up, smiled at Morris and he found himself smiling back. As she passed his desk to leave the classroom she bent down*. 'I wrote quickly because I want to see the fight,' she whispered. 'It's going to be the funniest fight in the history of fights.'

Morris suddenly realised that if he didn't start writing his words out quickly, he'd be the last one left in detention with an angry mob waiting outside. He didn't want to leave on his own. He grabbed his pen, flicked the dictionary to the A section and ran his eyes down the page waiting for a word to jump out at him.

'I won't be a moment.' Mrs Burn got to her feet and went to the door. 'Keep working until I get back.' And she left the classroom.

to bend down *herunterbeugen*

There was a thud* and then another as Calvin and his followers started banging on the window to frighten Morris.

Morris tried to concentrate on finding a good A word, but he couldn't. He got to his feet and went to the window. He smiled the most annoying* smile he could, one that he usually saved for his little sister, and pulled the blinds* down. On his way back to his desk, the other boy in detention, Toby, got up and put his piece of paper on Mrs Burn's desk.

'Tell Mrs Burn I finished.'

'That was quick.'

'Why are you surprised? Everyone's gathering in the park for the fight. I wouldn't miss this for the world.' And he left.

Morris sighed. Perhaps he should just accept his fate* and march towards his death like a brave soldier. Holly's plan seemed foolish* and doomed* to fail. He stared at the wall which was covered with Easter holiday assignments. While he was wondering what to do, he spotted* a

thud *dumpfer Schlag* | annoying *nervig* | blind *Jalousie* | fate *Schicksal* | foolish *töricht* | to be doomed to fail *zum Scheitern verurteilt sein* | to spot *entdecken, bemerken*

name he recognised*: Mary Porcus. He scanned*
her neat* handwriting and then quickly started
flicking through the pages of his dictionary. He
ran his finger down a page until he found the
word he was looking for:

Arachnophobia – extreme or irrational fear of
spiders.

11
Friday, 13th of June – 5 p.m.

As Morris wrote out his twenty-six words,
he wondered how he could best get past the
children waiting for him outside the English block.
There was a back way out of the building, but
when he didn't come out the front, he'd only have
a few minutes before they realised he'd chosen
the back door and there was a serious risk of him
getting trapped* by the bike sheds*.

'Think Morris,' he said to himself. 'That is one
thing you are actually good at.'

He handed his piece of paper to Mrs Burn, who
smiled and said he could go.

As he pulled on his coat and bag, he could see
eyes at the window peeping* round the edge*
of the blind. The children were watching and
waiting for him to leave.

He boldly* waved and smiled at them, before
calmly walking out of the classroom and into the
hall. He went to one of the broken lockers* and
quickly shoved his coat and bag inside. He needed

to get trapped *in eine Falle geraten* | shed *Schuppen* |
to peep *spähen* | edge *Rand, Kante* | bold *forsch, mutig*

to be able to run fast. He crept* to the front entrance of the English block and waited.

'Where is he?'

'He must have gone out the back,' someone said after a minute.

'Quick, let's get him!' someone else cried. There was a sound like stampeding* elephants as the gang* of kids hungry for blood ran around the back of the building.

Morris peered through the glass door. The playground was empty. He pushed the door open and ran as fast as he could across the playground towards the gate. Just as he reached it, he heard an angry shout.

'There he is!'

Morris pushed his nose up into a snout again and shouted, 'Catch me if you can baldy pig!' And then he ran for his life. He needed to make it to the end of the road and round the corner to Holly, who would be waiting by the gate of her grandad's garden.

locker *Schließfach* | to creep *schleichen, kriechen* | stampeding *wild geworden* | **gang** *Horde*

His breath came hard and his lungs felt tight*
as he sprinted, but he could hear the thunder
of running feet behind him and fear catapulted
him forwards. He felt like an antelope being
chased by a stampede of startled* bison.
He threw his chest forward and forced* his legs
to move faster. He needed to make it to the
gate. He ran around the corner. He could see
Holly, waving him towards her with an urgent
expression on her face. His breath was coming in
gasps and his throat was sore*, but as he sprinted
through the gate he managed* to gasp the word:
'Arachnophobia!'

Holly's face lit up and she laughed with delight*.
'Brilliant!' she replied, ushering him through the
gate. 'Quick, into the shed.'

Morris looked out across the garden. It had three
sections. The section near the house was raised*
flowerbeds full of vegetables separated* by wide
paths. The middle section was formal flower beds
and the bottom third of the garden, beside the
gate, was a wildflower meadow*. In the corner

---

tight *eng* | startled *aufgeschreckt* | to force *zwingen* | sore
wund | to manage *schaffen* | delight *Freude, Entzücken* |
raised *erhöht* | separated *getrennt, geteilt*

Morris spotted a rickety* shed covered in ivy*.
As he crossed the meadow he felt the splash of
thick raindrops falling from the sky. 'Oh, great!'
He looked up. 'Now it's raining.'

'Stop grumbling*.' Holly ran past him, grabbing
his jumper and pulling him towards the shed
as the gate swung* open. 'Rain won't hurt you.
In fact it might be to our advantage.'

'If you think I won't fight you in here, you're
wrong,' Calvin said, boldly marching into the
garden.

---

meadow *Wiese* | rickety *baufällig* | ivy *Efeu* | to grumble
meckern, motzen | **to swing (swung, swung)** *schwingen*

62

Holly pushed Morris into the shed, turning to stand in the doorway.

'I'm not scared of you, you big bully,' Holly called back, sticking out her chin. 'I brought you here, to the scene of your crime, so my grandad can have the pleasure of hearing you apologise* for smashing up his vegetables.'

Calvin threw back his head and laughed. 'Calvin Porcus doesn't apologise to anyone, ever.'

'We'll see about that,' Holly said, slipping* into the shed and closing the door.

to apologise *sich entschuldigen* | **to slip** *hier: huschen*

12

Friday, 13th of June – 6 p.m.

Inside the shed, Morris was still trying to catch his breath. He felt a spark* of panic in his chest. They were trapped. There was no way out, other than the door they'd come in. He looked around the shed wondering if Holly had filled it with awesome weapons, but all he could see were empty plant pots, a selection of rusty* tools and a box of seed* packets. The floor was so rotten that there were weeds* growing up through it in the far corner.

He heard Holly tell Calvin she was going to make him apologise to her grandfather and realised with a sinking feeling that she must be mad. There was nothing in this shed that would help them scare Calvin, and now they were trapped. The shed was surrounded* by at least thirty children all shouting for a fight and they had no way out. Morris was beginning to regret* pulling pig faces at Calvin. Why had he listened to Holly?

---

spark *Funke* | rusty *verrostet* | seed *Samen* | weed *Unkraut* |
to be surrounded *umzingelt sein* | to regret *bereuen*

She shut the shed door and bolted* it from the inside.

Morris peered out of the small square glass window at the crowd outside. He heard the light patter* of rain on the shed roof as the spectators* for the fight spread out into a semi-circle around the shed. Calvin was making a show of slowly rolling up his sleeves*.

'You can't stay in there forever,' he shouted.

'We are dead.' Morris turned to look at Holly. 'What on earth are you doing?'

Holly was bent over the weeds that were sprouting* up through the shed floor. She reached down and grabbed two tall nettle* stalks* at their base* and ripped* them out of the ground, laying them carefully on the workbench*. Then she squatted* down and picked up the large plant pots, looking inside them.

'I don't think this is the ideal time for gardening*!' Morris said.

to bolt *verriegeln* | patter *Prasseln* | spectator *Zuschauer* | sleeve *Ärmel* | to sprout *wachsen* | nettle *Nessel* | stalk *Stängel* | base *hier: Wurzel* | to rip *(heraus-)reißen* | workbench *Werkbank* | to squat down *hinhocken* | gardening *Gartenarbeit*

'I'm not gardening,' Holly said. 'I'm getting the weapons we need to teach that pig-headed bully a lesson.'

Morris frowned. This girl was definitely crazy. She was picking snails* and slugs* out of the plant pot and putting them into an empty seed tray. He glanced out of the window. Calvin was on the ground doing some push-ups*. The children were chanting his name over and over again.

'Come over here and help,' Holly scolded*. 'You are the one that got us into this mess. You have to be seen to be fighting, otherwise when this is all over, you'll still get bullied.'

'You don't think we can really win this fight,' Morris said. 'The boy out there is as big as a rhinoceros.'

'Yeah, but we know what he's afraid of.' Holly was grinning. 'And it's brilliant.'

'Spiders?'

'Spiders,' she nodded. 'A very common* fear as it happens which is crazy, particularly in England. There isn't a spider native* to this country that can seriously hurt a human, and they do so many important jobs in our homes and gardens, getting rid of* insect pests.'

'But, I don't understand. How are spiders going to help us?' Morris stared at Holly. 'Are you a spider whisperer?'

'A what?'

'You know, one of those people who can talk to animals by making some kind of special noise?'

Holly laughed. 'No, you idiot,' she shook her head. 'We are going to use spiders to teach Calvin that it is not nice to frighten other people. Once he's had a taste of his own medicine, he's going to apologise to my grandad.'

to scold *schimpfen* | common *geläufig, verbreitet* | native *einheimisch* | to get rid of *loswerden*

'I don't think he's going to do that. Even if we do manage to escape* with our lives, he'll never apologise.'

'He will when he meets Gertie.'

'Gertie? Who is Gertie?'

Holly pointed up into the corner of the shed. 'Gertie is a huge orb weaver spider*, and she's just had millions of babies.'

Morris looked up and saw lots of tiny yellow baby spiders clumped* in one section of a spider web.

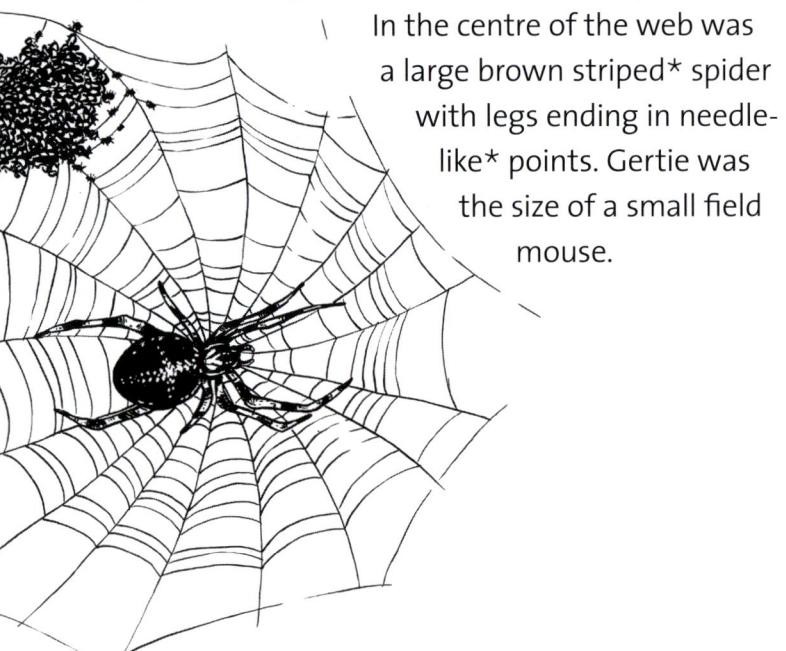

In the centre of the web was a large brown striped* spider with legs ending in needle-like* points. Gertie was the size of a small field mouse.

to escape *entkommen* | orb weaver spider *echte Radnetzspinne* | clumped *zusammengedrängt* | striped *gestreift* | needle-like *nadelähnlich*

13

Friday, 13th of June – 6.25 p.m.

'Are you ready?' Holly asked.

Morris nodded. His heart was still pounding in his chest.

'Remember to grasp the nettle firmly. That's the only way not to get stung*.'

There was a bang as something hit the wall of the shed. Calvin was becoming impatient*.

'Come out here and face your doom!' he shouted, and all the other kids yelped and jeered.

'This is your last chance,' Holly shouted. 'You can apologise to my grandad, Morris and me and leave quietly, or we are going to come out there and teach you a lesson.'

There was a roar of laughter. 'Never!' shouted Calvin.

Holly opened the bolts* of the shed door and strode out swinging a nettle like a sword.

to sting (stung, stung) *stechen, hier: (ver)brennen* | impatient *ungeduldig* | bolt *Riegel*

Calvin pointed and whooped. 'Oh no! She's going to fight me with a leaf*!'

She looked at Morris. 'GET HIM!' she shouted.

Morris reached into the small bag belted to his trousers and pulled out a snail. He put it into the sling shot* and fired it at Calvin.

Everything seemed to slow down as Calvin opened his mouth to shout an insult* at Holly and the snail sailed right into the open hole. Calvin's eyes opened wide and he doubled over* as he retched* and spat* the poor snail out. Holly ran forwards brushing the nettle across the back of his neck and he howled as he was stung.

Morris reached into his bag again, this time pulling out two slugs. One after the other he fired the slugs at Calvin. Both sailed passed Calvin

leaf *Blatt* | sling shot *Steinschleuder* | insult *Beleidigung* | to double over *sich krümmen* | to retch *würgen* | to spit (spat, spat) *spucken*

70

hitting the crowd of onlookers who all squealed and shuffled backwards. Morris felt hope and courage rise up in his chest. Quick as he could, he reloaded the sling and fired load after load of slugs and snails at Calvin and the onlookers, who quickly turned from a jeering audience to whimpering* children ducking to avoid* the snails.

Calvin was purple with rage*. He grabbed the nettle, yanking it out of Holly's hand and howling as his hands and forearms* were stung, but he no longer cared. He stormed towards Holly like an angry bull. She held her ground, as he grabbed her jumper.

'I'm going to make you regret* you were ever born,' he growled.

Holly smiled up at him sweetly and shook her head, first slowly and then like they do in shampoo commercials* to show how thick and glossy their hair is. Millions of tiny* yellow spiders let themselves down her face on their silken strings*, swinging out like they were on a merry-go-round.

whimpering *wimmernd* | **to avoid** *vermeiden, ausweichen* | **rage** *Wut, Zorn* | **forearm** *Unterarm* | **to regret** *bereuen* | **commercial** *Werbefilm* | **tiny** *winzig* | **silken string** *Seidenfaden*

'What the...?' Calvin stared at her trying to make sense of what was going on as at least five tiny spiders hit his face and started climbing up it. He yelled, letting go of Holly's jumper as Gertie the giant orb weaver climbed down her fringe* and onto her nose.

'Aaaaarrrrrrrgghhhhhhhhhhhhhh!' Calvin leapt backwards, as if the ground was burning his feet. He bumped against a kid who was cowering from the slug attack and fell to the ground.

'Spiders, all over your face,' the kid shrieked, pointing at the miniature mustard* arachnids crawling over Calvin's face.

fringe *(bei Haaren) Pony* | mustard *hier: senfgelb*

'Aaaarrrrrrrggghhhhhhhhhh! They're in my face!'
Calvin rolled over and over on the ground, his
hands hitting his face. 'Get them off.' He leapt
to his feet and started doing an odd dance. His
knees and elbows wobbled* about as he shook
his whole body trying to shake some imaginary
foe* off him. The children who had come to see
Morris get a beating* began to laugh and point
at Calvin.

Morris had run out of slugs and snails to fire,
so he grabbed the stalk of the nettle, sticking
out of his back pocket, like Holly had shown
him and waved it about in front of him like
a bendy sword*. The groups of frightened
children drew back a step. No one wanted to
get stung.

Holly reached up her two hands and cupped
them around the large spider on her nose,
lifting Gertie down. 'Aw, you're not afraid of a
little spider, are you?' She held out her hands
towards the trembling* Calvin.

'You win, you win!' he shrieked. 'Please, please,
don't bring that thing anywhere near me.'

to wobble *wackeln* | foe *Gegner, Feind* | beating *Prügel,
Schläge* | sword *Schwert* | to tremble *zittern*

14

Friday, 13th of June – 6.40 p.m.

'The party's over,' Holly called out to the group of spectators. 'Go home. No one is going to get hurt here today.'

'You heard her,' Calvin bellowed*. 'Go away.'

Some of the children ran out of the gate, relieved to get away from the slug and spider fight, others dragged* their feet, disappointed* that nobody was getting a nosebleed or black eye today.

Holly waited, holding the spider out in her closed hands as she watched them all file out* the gate.

'Can I go now too, please?' Calvin begged.

'Not until you've apologised to my grandad.' Holly looked at Morris. 'Is there anything you want to say to Calvin?' she asked him.

Morris waved his nettle. 'Do you promise to never ever try to beat me up again?'

'I promise,' Calvin cried.

'Swear* on your sister's life.'

---

to bellow *brüllen* | to drag *schleppen* | disappointed
enttäuscht | to file out *hintereinander heraus gehen* |
to swear *schwören*

'I swear on Mary's life.'

Morris felt a wave of relief and euphoria. They'd
won! They had actually beaten Calvin Porcus
in a fight! He dropped the nettle and looked at
Calvin's terrified face and immediately felt sorry
for him. He knew what it was like to be terrified.
'Listen,' Morris stepped forward and held out
his hand. 'I didn't want to pelt* you with slugs
and snails,' he said. 'It's just that I am as terrified
of you as you are of that spider. Can we shake
hands?'

'I was only going to rough* you up a bit,' Calvin
said, taking Morris's hand. 'I wasn't really going
to kill you. I was hoping if I terrified you enough, I
wouldn't have to. You know, you'd pee your pants
and fall on the floor sobbing* and I wouldn't
even have to swing a fist. That's what normally
happens.'

'Well, I'm sorry that I said that thing about your
name. I didn't realise that people would use it
to tease* you. I'm especially sorry about your
little sister. I mean, I'm not good at fighting, but
if anyone was mean to my little sister Sukie, I
would at least try to punch them.' Holly raised her

to pelt sb with sth *jdn. mit etw. bombadieren* | to rough sb
up *jdn. aufmischen* | to sob *schluchzen* | to tease *ärgern,
hänseln*

eyebrows and gave him a meaningful look. 'Oh yeah, and it wasn't Holly's idea to tell everyone about your name. When you asked me who had put me up to it, her name just popped out of my mouth. So you see, I got her into trouble and then you went and smashed up her grandad's vegetables, which is kind of my fault, too. Anyway, it's all a bit of a mess and I wanted you to know that I'm very sorry people have been mean to you and your little sister about your name.'

'You had nothing to do with any of this?' Calvin looked at Holly and she shook her head. 'Oh,' his head drooped*. 'I feel bad.'

'Good, then you won't mind coming and apologising to Grandad.' She held out her hands and Calvin scrambled to his feet, hurrying towards the house in front of her. When they got to the French doors she called out. 'Grandad, are you in there?'

Morris heard a merry* chuckle* and an elderly man with a grey and white beard rolled out of the doors in a wheelchair.

'Of course, I am my dear. Watching you was more fun than the television.'

to droop *hängen lassen* | **merry** *fröhlich* | **chuckle** *Kichern*

Calvin was blushing hard. 'I'm sorry, Sir, I ruined your vegetables. It was wrong. I wish I hadn't done it.' He looked at the old man's chair. 'Especially, as you are in a wheelchair.' He looked ashamed. 'I'm very sorry.'

'Well, young man, how do you suggest to set things right?'

'Erm,' Calvin looked at the raised flowerbeds and shrugged, 'I could help you plant new ones?'

'That is a very good idea.' Holly's grandad nodded.

'I think I should help, too,' Morris said. 'It was my fault that Calvin thought Holly had anything to do with any of this.'

'Excellent, two helpers for the garden! How wonderful,' he clapped his hands. 'We should have orange juice to celebrate. Holly, take poor Gertie back to her shed. She'll be terrified.'

15
August and later

Over the summer holidays, Calvin, Morris and Holly met in her grandad's garden several times a week. They weeded* and picked ripe* fruit and vegetables. They sowed* seeds and watered everything, including each other. Holly introduced Calvin to the insects in the garden and they built a bug hotel. Slowly, he grew less frightened of spiders and became fascinated by them. Holly showed him and Morris how plants have pests that eat them and how spiders and other insects eat the pests.

Morris was surprised to discover* that Calvin was kind and very clever. They swapped* book recommendations* and by the end of the summer the three of them had become good friends.

In early September, when it was time to return to school, Holly's grandad said that they had more than paid for their crimes against his vegetables,

---

to weed *Unkraut jäten* | **ripe** *reif* | **to sow** *säen* | **to discover** *entdecken, herausfinden* | **to swap** *austauschen* | **recommendation** *Empfehlung*

but that they were welcome in his garden anytime.

Morris was disappointed that he wouldn't be seeing his friends as often as before, but Calvin announced* that he wanted to keep coming after school and on Sundays, and they all agreed that there was too much work to do in the garden to leave it all to Holly's grandad. When they asked him if they could continue visiting and working in the garden, he was delighted to let them. He found the company of the young people rejuvenating*, and they enjoyed learning what he had to teach them about growing flowers, fruits and vegetables.

Some evenings they would sit down together after a few hours of working in the garden and eat some of their harvest*, and telling the story about the time that Holly had terrified Calvin with a spider wig*.

to announce *verkünden, ankündigen* | rejuvenating *verjüngend* | harvest *Ernte* | wig *Perücke*